"*i don't think *i'm straight*"

other works by the author:

*how sunflowers bloom under moonlight*
*how to be heartbroken.*
*how to be mentally well.*
*the letters i will never send.*
*deluded: a guide to situationships*

there's something
i need to tell
you …

# "i don't think i'm straight'

## isabella dorta

EBURY
PRESS

EBURY PRESS

UK | USA | Canada | Ireland | Australia
India | New Zealand | South Africa

Ebury Press is part of the Penguin Random House group of companies whose addresses can be found at global.penguinrandomhouse.com

Penguin Random House UK
One Embassy Gardens, 8 Viaduct Gardens, London SW11 7BW

penguin.co.uk

First published by Ebury Press in 2026

1

Copyright © Isabella Dorta 2026
Illustrations © Laura Martin 2026
The moral right of the author has been asserted.

No part of this book may be used or reproduced in any manner for the purpose of training artificial intelligence technologies or systems. In accordance with Article 4(3) of the DSM Directive 2019/790, Penguin Random House expressly reserves this work from the text and data mining exception.

Typeset in 11.5/15pt Garamond MT Pro by Six Red Marbles UK, Thetford, Norfolk

Printed and bound in Great Britain by Clays Ltd, Elcograf S.p.A.

The authorised representative in the EEA is Penguin Random House Ireland, Morrison Chambers, 32 Nassau Street, Dublin D02 YH68

A CIP catalogue record for this book is available from the British Library

ISBN 9781529958867

 Penguin Random House is committed to a sustainable future for our business, our readers and our planet. This book is made from Forest Stewardship Council® certified paper.

*to every woman
i have ever loved,*

*and to those i was too afraid to.*

*TW — homophobia, sexual assault, trauma,
self-harm, mental health*

please be aware that whilst there is a lot of joy and freedom in discovering your sexuality, there is also a hell of a lot of discomfort; of funny looks; of danger; of loss.

not every story is the same. not every queer person experiences acceptance. not every coming out ends happily.

like many, i have found peace in my community, i have found a home. and whilst i now feel no shame about putting my pronouns in my bio, or a gay sticker on my water bottle, sixteen-year-old me did.

this book is for her.

and for you, whoever you are.

# chapters

i. lost  1

•

ii. liar  37

•

iii. skin  65

•

iv. true  103

•

v. safe  153

*you may forget but
let me tell you
this: someone in
some future time
will think of us.*

—sappho n.d.

                    i
                  have
                    a
                 secret.

i will tell you,
soon.

      but i haven't even admitted it to myself yet.

i promise you will know—
everyone will know,

              soon.

lost

'i don't think i'm straight'

have my palms ever not been clammy?

anxiety-littered flesh,
all splotchy
and scared,
never not afraid of my own hands.

always the quiet one,
always the unseen.

i can make myself unwell if i think about it too hard.

isn't that something?

*lost*

oh how i long for the sort of peace
i know i am not built for.

a quiet life is what i'd like
but i know it is probably not what i deserve.

'i don't think i'm straight'

i think i look out of place.
i think i might've always looked out of place.

in my too-big blazer, my school shoes and my ponytail. i've never been

*cool.*

i think i'd like to be

*cool.*

i think i'd like to be anything,
anyone,
other than me.

*lost*

do you see it?
in the mirror?

do you see a fraud too?

someone ready to spend another day
pretending to like themselves?

i do.
it's all i see.

## 'i don't think i'm straight'

when it hurts, when i feel like i don't belong, when i wish i were anyone but myself, i fall back onto old habits. i fall back into things that are not quite bad enough to be considered self-harm, but they're definitely not kind.

I. *i drink too much.*

II. *i'm too scared of dying to actually do drugs,*
*but i think about it.*
*a lot.*

III. *i over eat,*
*or under eat,*
*depending on the day.*

IV. *i refuse to leave my bed,*
*i sit in the dark,*
*i rot into oblivion.*

and my personal favourite,

V. *i over sexualise.*

i undo the top button, roll the waistband of my skirt up a couple of times, fluff my hair in the mirror. i tell myself: the best way to be happy is to make someone else happy.

i ask them to do whatever they want to me.

letting men use me
does not make me feel better,

*lost*

but it does make me feel something.

it makes me feel useful.

and something is better than nothing.

'i don't think i'm straight'

/

quiet, aren't i?
easy to pull around,
i never fight back, i never kick up a fuss.

i make you feel powerful, don't i?

i make you feel bigger,
like you're worth something,
like the person you've always dreamed you could be.

fantasy is my middle name and i exist
only for your pleasure.

so,
you open me up.
legs first,
split me in half,
try to destroy me
to make yourself feel like more of a man.

and i lay there,
playing the perfectly ruined girl,
smiling with mascara running down freshly hit cheeks.
i make my chest rise and fall for you.

i'll moan your name,
or whatever you asked to be called.
i'll tell you that no one has ever made me shake like that,

*lost*

but if i'm honest,
you haven't really even made a dent.

you're nothing like you think you are.
empty hunger and shallow want,

is it not embarrassing to be so sure of yourself
and so wrong at the same time?

and i'd love to tell you all of this,
to get up after sex,
not a single hair out of place,
and show you just how little you have made me feel,

to stop feeding your ego,
to stop faking my orgasms,

i don't like it,
i don't enjoy it,
you're actually pretty bad at sex,

but i keep going back.
i don't know why i keep going back.

'i don't think i'm straight'

i've never felt comfortable
in the arms of a man.
i just know it's where i'm supposed to be.

*lost*

undress me.

i stink of tears and numbness and
my body hurts from not being held.

hands.
hands, please.
hold me and help me to forget.
kiss me and make me like myself,
just for a moment.
skin is warmer in the dark
and mine is asking to be pressed up against yours.

pause
just for a moment,
before your teeth cut into my thighs.
that breath is where my self-worth exists
unbothered,
unharmed.
you are going to make me feel better tonight.

i am important
only when i am useful.
and naked.

please make me useful.
please make me useful.

'i don't think i'm straight'

i am asking to be saved from myself
and i know
that no one can do it
but me,
but that won't stop me from asking.

strangers in nightclubs,
while my skirt hitches itself up
and my lipstick smudges.

first dates in pubs,
alcohol-fuelled, empty stomach kisses
with insecurities on full display.

carried home by someone i hope is nice,
but probably won't touch me as kindly as i'd like.

monday morning regret and shame and self-hatred.
friday night delusion and desperation and forgiveness

that i really should keep for myself.

*lost*

i am nothing but theirs to take—
theirs to own—
theirs to fuck.

this is not making love,
this is not even sex.
this is ownership,
in the least flattering way.

afterwards,
they are too disgusted
*to even touch me*,
too repulsed
*to even look at me*,

i am not even worth being owned.

'i don't think i'm straight'

because the funny thing about being raised without love,

is that you'd expect to not know how,

but really,
you don't know how to not.

*lost*

i think i realise now that
it doesn't matter who they *say* they are,
what type of man they *claim* to be.

these men are no different.
they all have the same bones,
the blueprints for hurting us.

they are fleeting.
i have borne witness to this
over and over and over.

i know this,
you know this,

we know they are only here
to temporarily own us,
to make their claims to our bodies,
to leave marks between both
our legs
and the folds of our brains.

we already know we are going to let them.
i know i will not stop their hands
from roaming onto the parts of me
that i would prefer to stay hidden.

these men are fleeting.
how we will feel after they discard us,

will not be.

'i don't think i'm straight'

i don't want to wake up.

i want to sleep and sleep and sleep
and i don't want to wake up as me again.
i'd be happier as anyone else.

i hate myself.
i really do.

i hate how i look and how i act and how i love
and i hate that i always feel so out of place.

i don't belong.
anywhere.

i'm not sure that i'm built for living,

*lost*

i'm pretending
to be someone
i'm not

and i still hate myself.

i don't know how to not.

'i don't think i'm straight'

you'll pity me if i tell you what i really think of myself,

so i don't.

i give you glimpses,
moments where the mask slips,
little pockets of realness
and fear

and i let you in.

for a moment,
for a split second,
you get to see how much unhappiness is in my body.

you can touch the desperation,
dry my tears, stroke my face.
hold me, tell me you never knew i felt like this.

you'll wish i'd told you sooner,
you'll do
*anything*
to make sure i don't feel like this again.

your promises are so sweet,
i almost forget to hide myself away again.
almost.

then *click*.
as quick as you found me, i'm gone.
i'll take your hands off of me

*lost*

and i'll smile,
like nothing has ever been wrong.
i'll tell you it was just a moment of weakness,
a blip.

you'll second guess,
keep an eye on me on nights out, for weeks after.
you'll ask me how i'm doing,
but with a little too much sincerity to be mistaken as
small talk.

maybe you'll try to tell yourself
you never saw anything in the first place,
that it really was just *'one of those days'*

and you'll decide that i'm probably fine,
just a normal amount of depressed
and not worth worrying about.

but we'll both know.

we'll both know what you saw.

'i don't think i'm straight'

keep it hidden.
bury it.
never acknowledge how it hurts.

hide the real you.
hide the parts of you that no one would accept.

be brave,
be kind,
be what everyone else needs you to be,
but never ask them for anything in return.

not even when you're desperate.

*lost*

because kindness hurts
when you are the only one
spoon-feeding it
into you own mouth.

'i don't think i'm straight'

i have a lot of big feelings,
a lot of the time.

i'm what you would probably call
*dramatic*.

but all i do
is care too much
and worry nonstop.

all i want
is relief
from my emotions,
from my thoughts.

*lost*

my anxiety controls me.

i can hear it,
whirring.
the sound keeps me up at night,

and the overthinking ruins me.

it's self-sabotage,
backstabbing prophecies
and nightmares i hope won't come true.

i'm my own puppet.
and it's all about control.

'i don't think i'm straight'

and just as we always hope it won't,
death finds us out of nowhere.

death does not discriminate.
there is no bargaining, no escape,
no way to avoid the human experience
that is grief.

i have lost something,
something that i had just yesterday,
that i had on the page before this one
and always took for granted.

i am grieving,
i am distraught,

i am shrivelling and inconsolable.

i have lost someone who meant so much to me
and now the only thing i can do

is feel it all over.

*lost*

i miss you like
nothing i've ever missed before.

and yet,
it is easier to just
not.

to pretend i have forgotten how my chest hurts
and not let myself feel any of it.

if i grieve, you are gone.
you really are gone.

'i don't think i'm straight'

there are people that rely on me,
to be strong and lovely,
so i brush it all aside,
save my tears for the pillow,
move on and cope and be less of a burden.

i bottle it all up,
shove it all the way down
and say the words *'i promise i'm okay'*
enough times to want to be sick.

i'm not sure if people actually believe me,
or if they just can't be bothered to prod any deeper,
but i don't have to unpack my grief
and they don't have to deal with my snotty crying,
so it's smiles all round.

i don't process,
i don't feel,
i don't accept.

i know things like death need to be felt at some point,
i know future me will probably be pissed off
when the inevitable grieving
rears its ugly head during a very inconvenient time,

but not now.
i can't right now.
driving home after another horrible hookup,

*lost*

the radio plays the same song we did at your funeral.

i see you in the rearview mirror.

you sit behind me. buckled in.
you smile that very alive, very gap-toothed smile.
i blink.
and you're gone as quick as you left the first time.

'i don't think i'm straight'

it's trickling in now,
slowly,
but i feel the chill creeping down the collar of my shirt.
i ignore it,
or at least,
i try to.

daffodils begin to bloom
and i want to rip them out.
my flatmate bakes a loaf of bread
and i hope she burns it.

i have to wash some of your dirty clothes.
i don't want to.

i see your favourite coffee mug
every time i go to make a cup of tea and it takes everything
in me not to smash it to shit.

i don't think i'm doing very good at this grieving thing.

*lost*

i think it might be my fault that you're dead.

if only i'd called you more,
watched where my feet fell on the paving,
prayed harder,
and meant it,
maybe you'd still be here.

maybe my overthinking deserved to be listened to
some more.
maybe i could've seen this coming
and done something different.
maybe it's all my fault.

maybe not,
maybe it's all in my head,
but self-loathing is easier than sorrow
and someone has to be held responsible.

'i don't think i'm straight'

i'm doing the washing one morning, about three weeks after you have passed, when it hits me. when i feel the air rush out of me and the ground run away from under me. i realise very suddenly that the air in my apartment has not been warm since you left.

it is only now that i look around and see how empty this home is without having something worth coming home to. i sit on a sofa that is very empty and watch a tv that only plays empty shows and drink from mugs that are full, but taste empty.

and it is everything i never understood grief to be. new and unbearable, and all i have left of you. it is comfortably uncomfortable. oh all there is, is grief. i had not realised the metallic taste in my mouth was sadness until this very moment and now i cannot feel a single one of my fingers. there are more tears on my face than words that i know and my rib cage feels too small for my body.

i reach for my phone before i realise that i do not want to share this moment with absolutely anyone. this is mine. this little pocket in time is mine and no one else's. no one needs to see how i grieve or cry or relive you. no one but us needs to know of how i loved you.

this morning belongs to us.

i stroke circles on the inside of my arm and think of how i miss holding your little face. i almost feel guilty for enjoying

*lost*

how this grief hurts, but there is very little i have left of you to enjoy now. i let the tears run and my spine shake and i hold onto the pot of your ashes like i want to embed you into my skin forever. i hope that if i hold onto you for long enough, my hands may forget how to open, that they may remember how warm love is and decide to never let go.

i know i have not reinvented grief, but it is hard in this moment to imagine that anyone has ever felt this much.

'i don't think i'm straight'

i will never outlive this loss.
forever.
forever with me.

*lost*

you knew everything about me.
you were the only person to see me truly.
you knew things before i ever had to say them.
you knew me and you memorised me and you loved me
like nobody had ever loved me
and i've lost you.

you're gone and it doesn't make sense and why aren't you here and where can i go to find you?

is this grief?
is this grief?

'i don't think i'm straight'

pain and loss and grief and pretending—
i hold all of this.

and my biggest fear?
admitting that i have become everything
they expected me to be.

*lost*

slowly, i start to cope again.
it takes its time, but healing does find me.

i'm sad and it's not just because i miss you.
i eat and i can taste food properly again.
i laugh and i don't feel guilty.

i still ache,
i still cry.
i don't forget.

i hold you with me,
as tightly as ever,
but my hands are opening
and ready to hold onto something else, too.

liar

'i don't think i'm straight'

i am searching for a husband.
or a boyfriend.
or a whatever.

i am searching for a whatever.

a something, a someone. a way to feel like less of a loser, like i could be desired and special and not a disappointment to my parents. i am looking for my prince charming, my disney-esque love story, the future father of my children.

i don't really want children,
if i'm honest.

i'm sort of scared of the whole 'giving birth' thing? and the actual raising of the children. it all sounds a bit restrictive, like i'd have to give up everything i've ever worked for, like my life would become inconsequential, and lost in the noise of my baby's crying.

i'm not sure i'd be a very good mum,
or wife.

i don't think i'm selfless enough.

*liar*

because men do tend to ask a lot of us,
don't they?

women give up their stretch mark-free bodies
and their mouths
and their time

and men?

men give up what?
a man cave?
watching the football at the pub on a sunday?

they keep their stomach muscles intact
and their hormones no more erratic than usual
and we,
we have to deal with all the shit.

we get up in the middle of the night,
shoulders covered in vomit stains and sleep.
it's our nipples that get pulled on
and bitten.
*bitten!?*
can you imagine if a man had to breastfeed?
there'd be robots built with perky areolas
and milk-warming sensors.

we sacrifice everything.
and somehow, for some men,
it's still just never enough.

'i don't think i'm straight'

and he raises his voice at me again
and he does not apologise
and suddenly,

i am fourteen again.

and my dad
has not spoken to me in weeks
and my first boyfriend
is sulking
because i won't suck his dick
and my history teacher
is doing a really bad job of pretending
he isn't looking down my top.

and i realise that he is

just.
another.
man.

he is just another man
damaging just another woman,
feigning innocence
in courtroom after courtroom.

he is trying to hurt me
and i don't think he has failed.

*liar*

i bet they get off on it,
hurting women,

i bet it makes them
feel something.

i want to feel something.
i'd do anything to feel something.

they took all of that away from me.
i'm just a shell now.

'i don't think i'm straight'

give me normality and
bless me with the gift of being like everyone else.
let me blend, oh,
let me blend.

bitten lip, bloodied tooth, afraid tongue.
i am hurt, both inside and out,
worryingly irreparable,
past the point of no return.

damaged.

i'm just damaged.

that's it. that's the only way to say it.
there are no frills,
no fancy words to soften the blow.

i can try to make it pretty,
but it won't make me any easier to love.

*liar*

i don't feel entitled
to experience
a healthy love.

i don't think i deserve it.

how can i?
when all that men have ever done is abuse me?

'i don't think i'm straight'

cheated on.
hit.
spat at.
abused.

can you tell me your earliest memory of being
catcalled?

in your school uniform?
a man in a white van leering at you?
a husband pushing a pram into a bush, because he's too
preoccupied with your training bra tits?

do you feel it?
the worry?

every woman has stories.
plural.
every woman can tell you about the shame,
the embarrassment.

because it feels like our fault,
doesn't it?
it feels like fire-bound wrists and
buckets of water placed just out of reach

and news reporters,
asking why we didn't call for help sooner.
fear is often mistaken for anger.

*liar*

sadness is often mistaken for anger.

pain is often mistaken for anger.

i am not angry.

and when you think about having children,
and when you tell people
you're not sure if it's for you,

do you think about being terrified to have a
son?

to raise a man not too dissimilar
to the ones you already know?
worry that all you'd be doing is adding to the problem,
adding to yet another statistic.
you already feel ashamed
for the way he will emotionally torture women.
and that is wishful thinking,
to assume he will not also hurt them physically.

or do you think about being terrified to have a daughter?

because she will only ever face
the same hurt that you have.
the same misogyny, pay gap, hatred.
the name-calling and the constant fear of danger.
she will be subject to the same fate that you have
and there will be nothing you can do to stop it.

so what scares you more?
having a son?
or having a daughter?

*liar*

i hate them.
men.

i hate that i'll have to marry one eventually.

i've never liked how they look at me.
i've never liked looking at them.

'i don't think i'm straight'

i think i'm a little bit of a fraud, if i'm honest.

i've always felt like one.
i'm a feminist who seems to be threatened
by other women,
and i date men,
although i'm not sure i want to.

it's just all i know,
all i've been told i'm supposed to want,
i've had my future planned out for me
for longer than i've been able to walk.

i don't want anything more,
i wouldn't even know what more looks like.

i'm disappointment enough already,
i'd never hurt my parents like that,
would i?

*liar*

i look at her
and i think
*'she is everything that i'm not.'*

she's the cool girl.
the petite and attractive girl.
the men-prefer-her girl.

she's the reason i hang bedsheets over my mirrors.
the reason my tinder only has photos from the neck up.
the reason i cannot touch my own skin in daylight.

she is what gold looks like on a good day,
the summer breeze we hold our faces towards.
she is interlocking fingers
and palms that don't sweat.

she is freshly washed cotton bedsheets,
closed curtains,
a cold room with a warm heavy blanket.
a yellow-toned lamp,

a vanilla-scented candle,
that was probably on offer
and is definitely the best-smelling thing
you have ever bought.

she is what i dream of.
she is what i wish i was.

'i don't think i'm straight'

she is everything—
absolutely everything—

i am not.

*liar*

lights turned off,

the shower steam stops me from having to hate myself,

i can barely see my own skin.

and how pleasant it is to forget.

'i don't think i'm straight'

it's all in the small things.

how i push food round my plate,
how i order a starter while everyone else orders a burger,
how i ate earlier,
how i drink my green tea,
how i clasp my fingers around my wrist and wring myself
silly.

i am not okay.

i tell no one
and everyone.

i am too much body to be happy, or normal
and i must lose some of it.
i am shedding this skin
and praying i will turn into someone more beautiful,
someone easier to love,

someone who is not such a disappointment
to my friends.

i think they are saints for still liking me at this size.
i know i am unkind when i am starving
but i am hungry for something smaller.
life will be better when i am smaller,

won't it?

*liar*

too little of me worth loving
and yet
too much of me to love.

how devastating the truth is.

'i don't think i'm straight'

chipped pedicures,
mascara-smudged waterlines.
i see beauty in other women's mistakes.

hip dips and back roll imprints,
flecked skin and chapped lips.
flaws

that i've never liked on myself,
but obsess over
on anyone who's not me.

oh these
mystical, magical things,
these women.
beautiful in ways i have always wished i was.

*liar*

i have a reoccurring dream, it finds me monthly.

i wake, in my childhood bedroom, with fairy lights still on and a tulle canopy draped from the ceiling. i have no dark circles, no aching limbs, not even sleep in my eyes. i am well-rested, the floor is warm with sun, i have slippers placed by my bed. i sit up, not even needing to stretch, and watch how the light pours itself into every corner of my room, puddling in between the teddy bears, and the barbie dolls.

life is good. sweet.

and then i see my reflection in the mirror.

fingers find my face and feel skin. smooth, stretched out over jawbone, not a blemish in sight. there are eyelashes falling over each other and freckles delicately placed. my hands are pink, moisturised. my nails naturally grown, with the whites white enough to dazzle. i make eye contact with my stomach, and i don't flinch. thighs un-touching, calves turning obviously into ankles, feet un-swollen and un-veined.

i can't see a single feature to hate.

my breathing hitches, heart almost stops beating. i blink and feel thick lashes slowing my lids down. right here, right now, i love myself the way i have always wanted to.

i am worth loving, i am enough to be proud of, i am beautiful and unflawed and perfect and

then i wake up.

'i don't think i'm straight'

there is an ache inside of me.

it is desperate and starving,
bubbling over and ready to reveal itself
at any moment given.

i think i know that it's always been there.

i've felt it clawing at the sides of me,
skin tearing with lust.

something is happening here, whether i like it or not.
but for now, i have silenced it.
i have entombed it.

i have bandaged any obvious wounds
and hidden my insides from anyone
who might be looking.

i am doing my best to hide the struggle.

*liar*

brand me with that hot rod that spells liar,
mark me
and let me hear the pain
i have only ever felt
sizzle.

i want to smell the sin burning out of me,
if this is harm, so be it,
i have harmed myself enough already.

i have lied and pretended and cried—
this is not a confession,
no, far from it—
this is barely acknowledgement.

i will not admit my wrongdoings,
but i think of them often.

ashamed is too weak of a word.

'i don't think i'm straight'

train window poetry,
supermarket sushi,
orange tulips needing a water change
and scuffed lips.

loss is loitering here,
she is doing a bad job of hiding herself.

i am waiting for the drop—
help me try to predict the moment it will all come
crashing down.
when, not if,
everything becomes real,
becomes something i can no longer ignore,
i will feign surprise.
i will act as if i did not see it coming.

this lie has been sweet,
but i suppose i am not,
so let the truth come out as kindly as you can.
please.

*liar*

there is a lump in the back of my throat
and i cannot cough it up.
i have not even bothered to try yet.
i push it off,
like some chore i'm not ready to do yet.

i'm afraid of choking,
of spitting up and upsetting
everyone around me.

i don't want to be an inconvenience,
so i stay quiet.
i suffer—
oh,
i suffer.

'i don't think i'm straight'

keep it hidden.
don't let anyone see.

you don't want to be hated,
do you?

*liar*

i'm scared.

you know what i'm scared of,
don't you?

can you see through me like i think you can?
can you place the words hiding in the back of my throat
onto your tongue
and do the hard bit for me?

say what i am too scared to say,
please?
claim it for me.

'i don't think i'm straight'

i have a secret
that i'm too scared to tell you about yet,
but i will soon.

i promise i will tell you soon.

skin

## 'i don't think i'm straight'

so i'm at this party, and i'm sat on the sofa, and she's perched on my lap, and i think we're being discreet, but then the boys come over. lips sticky with cider, they pull us apart. they kiss us and the alcohol ensures it is not gentle. they are marking their territory, but her legs are still touching mine.

someone, somewhere, comments that we look very close and that we are flushed and blushing and that maybe she should sit on top of me again. they are asking for a show, so we give them one.

we are wearing matching outfits, so i accidentally forget where her lips end and mine begin and this kiss goes on past the cheers and the camera phone flash lights and the music doesn't actually stop, but for me it does. her rings dig into my neck and my boyfriend lets go of me and i cup her chin kinder than either of us have ever felt.

they want us to stop. i know they want us to stop, it's been going on too long to still be just a little bit of fun, but i don't care.

later, when i am home and i have already fought with my boyfriend, i tell myself it was just the alcohol, that i wouldn't do that sober, that i didn't enjoy it that much.

he doesn't believe me.

and i don't believe me either.

*skin*

'i don't think i'm straight'

softer,
with gentle touch
and burning skin.

i am marked—
changed.

bubbling in throats, bile-coated kisses
still taste sweeter
with her,
than any with him.

reliving this
on replay
nightly,

i am changed
for better or for worse.

nothing could ever be the same
after knowing such tender hands.

*skin*

and then the shame invites itself in.
and the self-loathing.

and you think it might just be a healthy mix of a hangover
and anxiety and fighting with your boyfriend and not
speaking to your best friend in over twelve hours,

but you know better.

you know you have to come to terms
with what you have always known,
but never dared to say out loud.

'i don't think i'm straight'

they watched us—
our boyfriends,
and then some.

they thought it was hot.
we thought that it made us cool.
(and also, we secretly wanted to know
what it would feel like,
to give into everything we knew we shouldn't.)

and that was all i had ever wanted to be really—
cool and fun
straight and my boyfriend's perfect girlfriend.

as long as he liked it,
i was happy to oblige and press my tongue against hers.

the first girl i kissed wasn't for me.

but underneath the embarrassment,
beneath the alcohol warmth and the peer pressure,
i kissed her and knew i liked it.

i kissed her and knew that kissing him had never felt like that.

*skin*

every time he touched me after she did,
kissed me after she did,
fucked me like i wished she had,
it solidified what i had hoped it wouldn't.

it wasn't right if it wasn't her.

so,
i had to pretend.

it's not like i hadn't had to before,
but i had never felt anything even close to what she had
given me back then.

it was easy to fake it
when i didn't know
what the real thing
was like.

'i don't think i'm straight'

because if there is one thing i can do,
it is perform.

give me any silly man and i will make him feel like a

*god.*

*skin*

eyes shut.
tight.
then opened,

whites wild and sheets rucked.
my lipgloss on his teeth.
body hair obliterated with lasers and sharp things and sweet and sticky things.

make up
oh so carefully smudged.

people pleaser,
performer,
porn star in the making.

loud brain that won't shut up.
sex hair.
pillow under my pelvis.
bitten neck.

fingers caught on his back's stretch marks.

wincing when they're not looking—
pleasure wincing when they are.

panting and painful,

'i don't think i'm straight'


tears
but only the sort he likes.

pretty and pinkish—
cool girl,
fun girl,
never complains too much girl.
sex doll girl.
cums at the same time that he cums girl,
every
single
time.

and
somehow,
he never questions it.

*skin*

i don't enjoy sex with men.
are we supposed to?
is it not all for them?
everything i have ever seen has told me
without words,
that sex,
is theirs.

we are warm and soft and malleable
and theirs.

don't tell me it is meant to be fun?
am i meant to enjoy it?

'i don't think i'm straight'

i think of her,
when he lays me down.
i think about women and breasts and her fingers
and where i'd like them to be placed.

i close my eyes
and he'll be pleased with himself for causing me
*so much pleasure,*

but it is easier to see her face in the dark.
i think of her and i start to feel something.
i start to see stars.

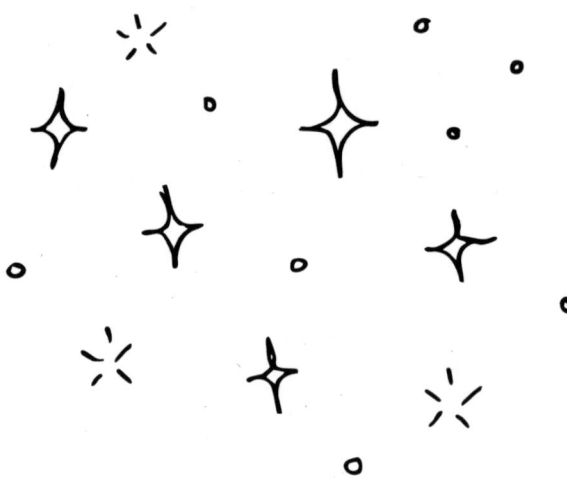

*skin*

she cannot know. ever.

she cannot know how much she has made me feel,

it would ruin everything.

## 'i don't think i'm straight'

we talk,
like girls do.

we are best friends,
seventeen and boy crazy—
well,
one of us is.

we share one blanket,
like we have always done.
her toes under my thigh, hands clasped around arms,
shoulder now renamed head rest, i cannot remember what i
ever used it for before.

her eyes.
her eyes are—
they look so pretty from the side.

and she tells me about this boy in her maths class and
i tell her that he definitely likes her back
and i stroke her hair
and she sleeps in my arms
and we are best friends.

we are just best friends.

*skin*

i think i need her.
oh, i think i need her like water.

'i don't think i'm straight'

but it is not just
her.

it is not just her lips and her touch and her body,

it is the idea of
women,

the very essence of how they
love.

it is all i think about.

*skin*

i feel consumed,
and not in a good way.

i breathe and taste this sin in my mouth
and i am not religious in the slightest
but i'm still sinning, aren't i?

i'm still thinking about sinning
and thinking about sinning
and thinking about sinning

and thinking about touching her
and thinking about kissing her
and thinking about loving her

and i really don't want to admit it,
but i really want to do it.

'i don't think i'm straight'

fear has a hold of my hands
and this body is stone cold—

clawing inside of me to be let out,
desire calls for me.
it calls for love,
warmth,
breathlessness.

it is louder, still.

let me find peace on a bed that i do not own.
i will cook us girl dinner to eat
on laid tables,
with flower tablecloths and pink plates
and i will kiss your lipstick mouth clean.

oh is this wrong?
is this wrong
is this wrong?

*skin*

and one night,
one unassuming, one not very special night,
after weeks of quiet yearning,

she places her hand on my cheek.

she
places her hand
on my
cheek.

i fall into her body
and pulses shift uncomfortably
until they are raging in ears.

hot breath, shaking fingers, hair brushed out of face.
something unstoppable has started.

## 'i don't think i'm straight'

i was not prepared for how good this would feel.
without watchful eyes
or alcohol-hazed vision.

i have imagined this for so long,
fallen asleep hot and bothered and with my thighs twisted together.
i have pretended to touch and stroke my own hair
and my own body
and yet nothing,
*nothing,*
has ever come close to this.

i squirm and i sigh and i moan.

*skin*

if she took her hands from my waist
i think my guts might just spill out.

my skin clearly cannot be trusted.
red and embarrassed,
sensitive and pleading for all of hers,

i will empty myself on the floor in front of her—

shoes—and friendship—
ruined quicker than you
can say '*more,*
please.*'*

containing this feels impossible.
how did i contain this for so long?

'i don't think i'm straight'

and she kisses me again.
and she kisses me again.
and she kisses me again.

and

how sweet it is,
to finally give in
to everything

you have ever thought about being.

*skin*

sticky skin pulls as we separate,
eyes looking downwards
and regret lashing at our throats.

shame pushes itself into my chest,
and i want to dry heave with guilt.
oh what have i done?

i have unleashed something untamable,
ruined my chances of a normal, happy life.

i have tasted bliss
and now nothing less than this
will ever come close
to satisfying me.

reckless,
how reckless of me

to let in just enough light to blind me,
everything looks different now,
my future entirely new.

i see it,
i hate it,
and i want it.

'i don't think i'm straight'

embarrassment spreads in bodies like wildfire.
it catches
and refuses to let go.
it finds you in the middle of the night,
at two pm in a classroom,
on the sofa on sundays.

you cannot outrun it.

you must face it head on.
you must look yourself in the eyes
and admit you do not hate yourself.

thinking about fucking girls
will not ruin you.
it is not the dagger you imagine it is.
you do not have to die on this hill.

i promise you,
acceptance feels better than this.

*skin*

it's moments like these that make me realise how much
i miss you.

i have things i wish i could tell you,
so many things.

i'm scared.

i have no one else.
mum won't understand,
dad might kick me out.
you would have hugged me.
you would have helped me.

you always made me feel normal.

'i don't think i'm straight'

why am i so afraid to just
be me?

why can't i live and love as i want to?

*skin*

i want it and i could cry and cry and i am desperately scared. i cannot tell anyone. no one would understand, no one has ever felt the same— i am alone and weird and pining and i want to brush hair off of her face. no. no.

no. help me, please? help me rid myself of this desire, i cannot do this. i am yearning and it hurts it hurts it hurts. i have never needed something so badly.

i am sure i am crazy.

'i don't think i'm straight'

just a one-time thing.
just a little bit of fun,
just a casual, never-again experience.

but does it have to be?
does this have to be the only time i feel skin
as soft as my own,
as exfoliated and cared for on a sunday?

could i bottle this and keep it?
enjoy the gentle tingling
and learn to not feel so ashamed
at how much i want to touch another woman?

she is lovely
but this is bigger than her.
she has merely opened the floodgates
and whether she meant to or not,
i am beginning to drown.

*skin*

i wonder if it is even the being gay that scares me,
or the funny looks that come along with it.

because yes,
women are quite scary,
but men are what
keep me up at night.
men are what i pray
i will not run into
on the walk home,
men are what
i am afraid of.

they look at me like i am meat enough already,
but i know of how they fetishise,
how i will come out,
not as gay to them,
but as their next secret meal,
their next piece of porn.

i am a fantasy.
i am a misogynist's wet dream.
i am in the closet and i am too afraid

to let the light in

'i don't think i'm straight'

because with light,
comes vulnerability,
comes being seen.

and i am not sure if i am ready for that yet.

*skin*

but what does 'ready' mean
anyway?

what do i need to do
to be ready

to admit
this secret?

this thing inside of me,
that's burning

and making holes
in my body?

'i don't think i'm straight'

this has found me rather quickly,
but then again,
i think it was always
here,

puddling at my feet,
waiting for
quiet acknowledgement,

some crack of light
to grow
towards.

i have held it
back
for so long,

oh how it hurts to let this part of me grow.

i am petrified
of someone finding out,
but i am so tired of
hiding.

i'm so tired of hiding this love.

*skin*

can i bury this?

can i look away
and pretend
that i have not caught a glimpse of this
in the mirror,
every morning
since learning of my own reflection?

is this salvageable?
could i keep pretending
and avert my eyes
of every pretty girl who walks into the room?

oh there are so many pretty girls.
oh i am so sick of pretending.

'i don't think i'm straight'

this *thing* inside of me,
this craving, this need,
this secret.

it is not going anywhere,
but out.

*skin*

i suppose it might be time to be honest with myself.
i hope it is not too late,
i hope there is still time to live.

'i don't think i'm straight'

i track my mother down,
in between lunch and dinner.
my hands shake as i stir sugar into tea,
one for me,
two for her.

she pauses the show she's watching.
confused,
slightly annoyed,

she doesn't get much time to herself on tuesdays
and i am disrupting
a rather animated discussion
on *the real housewives of beverly hills.*

she does not understand why i look so scared.
she asks me what i want.

i think about saying,
*'for you to not hate me,'*
but instead,
i say—

*skin*

'i need to tell you something.

'i don't think i'm straight.'

true

'i don't think i'm straight'

is that it?
am i out?
is it all over?

has the sky come crashing down
and everyone i've ever loved disowned me?
it hasn't?

i'm still scared.
i'm still so scared.

*true*

the morning after i came out to my mum,

i woke up and my curtains still opened the same
and the sun still felt comfortable

throwing herself into my room
and my bedding still felt soft as it held me.

i didn't die from the shame.
i didn't suddenly become undeserving
of life
or of love.

i did cry
and she did look at me differently
and it wasn't easy,

but i didn't die.
i'm still here.

she still brought me up a cup of tea
and a slice of toast for breakfast
like she does every morning.

she told me
she'll get over it eventually,
probably.
she said it's just a shock,
to think about never having '*real*' grandchildren.

she's asked me not to tell my dad just yet.

'i don't think i'm straight'

i wish i had been born different.

it would all be so much easier
if i was not
me.

*true*

i decide that, for now, telling one person is enough.

the weight is lighter,
burden slightly lifted,
secret shared,
even if it wasn't exactly welcomed.

i know what everyone at school thinks of me.
i know how they smirk at me when my back is turned.
pointed comments and snide remarks
and judgements better left unsaid,
i know how bad things would be if they found out.

for now, i stay hidden. for now.

'i don't think i'm straight'

the thing about hiding is,
if you do it well enough,
you'll forget who you really are.

*true*

desperate to be normal,
and straight,
and less of an outcast.

so many years of telling myself false truths,
i think i even started to believe it.
i kidded myself well enough,
for long enough,

i started to believe that i actually liked men.

and so now,
to finally know what's true,
to admit to myself
everything i've always been too scared to admit,
i feel like a fraud.

this queerness was impossible to ignore,
but i still feel like a liar
and i still don't really know
who i am.

'i don't think i'm straight'

weeks pass,
and i am still technically not out yet,
and i am restless.

nothing has changed,
but everything has changed.

i drop hints with close friends,
i share posts on social media,
i cosplay as just an ally,

i hope for someone to just outright ask me,
take the pressure off of me and just assume,
to save me from shocked faces,
or worse,
disgusted expressions.

*true*

it begins as an itch.
most definitely noticeable,
but easy to ignore if you try hard enough.

like when you're pretending to be
asleep on the drive home,
hoping you might shut your eyes tight enough
to be carried to bed by your dad.

and you almost manage to forget about it,
but then it burns.
aches.
gouges.
rips.

it begs to be acknowledged.
it will not leave you alone.
it does not lighten up.

this is what i try to tell my mum,
when she asks why
i couldn't just keep this sin
to myself.

i wish i would have.

'i don't think i'm straight'

i watch queer movies in secret,
on repeat,
to try to purge the desire out of me.

i think i thought if i watch it enough,
i won't want to act on it.

it doesn't really work,
because all it makes me want to do
is kiss another woman.

it just makes me sad.

*true*

the anger comes later,
hot and fast.
it's the sort that makes your forehead vein throb—

i want to kill someone.
maybe myself,

maybe the next person to call me a dyke.

if only they knew.
oh if only they knew.

'i don't think i'm straight'

all i want
is to be someone
not bothered by their opinions.

all i am
is bothered.

*true*

to be unashamed.
to live as me.
to love another woman.
to be free.
to touch her shin with mine. in bed.
to laugh.
to cry.
to laugh and cry.
to eat a wedding cake with lesbian cake toppers.
to kiss in public without fear.
to have a soft hand to hold.
to feel peace.
to finally be happy.
to love.

—why i want to come out.

'i don't think i'm straight'

i think i might scream about it.
anything would feel better than quiet,
than pretending
and silently living.

i don't want to be hidden forever,
i need everyone to know and
i need them to know now.

*true*

i tell the world.
i tell everyone.
i tell instagram.

i come out and it is nothing like i imagined it to be.
no youtube reveal party, no public declaration,
no tears, no strangers hugging me,

just a stupid instagram post,
but it feels so good.

i almost forget to be scared.

'i don't think i'm straight'

oh what a rush!
what a rush to be free!

hello, hi, world,
do you hear me?
i'm here, i'm right here,
spinning with you,
catching a ride through the universe!
we are moving and twirling and i am here!
alive!

i'm here!

*true*

the phrase
*'queer joy'*
has never made so much sense.

i step foot
into my first lesbian bar,

i add my pronouns
to the end of every email,

i cut my hair
and paint my nails green

and swap underwire
for comfort.

i read poetry
about pomegranates

and buy
my first carabiner.

i stock up on jorts
and baby tees
and hair clips.

'i don't think i'm straight'

i listen to girl in red
and blush at the bridge in
'bad idea!'

nothing is sweeter
than facing the thing
that has been holding
you back
for your entire life.

nothing says healing like facing it head on.

*true*

'i don't think i'm straight'

no matter what i do
to drown it out,
i can never manage to silence
the voice in my head.

it says everything i've
never wanted to hear.

*true*

the novelty does eventually
wear off.
like most things,
the excitement dies down.

it becomes normal,
not always accepted,
sometimes interrogated,
but normal.

i fade back out of the spotlight
and colleagues and friends
seem to forget
what i am.

but i don't.

don't be fooled,
i might look like i'm not petrified,
like i'm so sure of myself,

but i still sit up in the mornings,
hands outstretched and eyes searching,

checking i'm still gay,
just in case.

'i don't think i'm straight'


self-doubt is something i cannot leave behind.

i carry it with me always.

*true*

i stay somewhat
surface level.

i don't yet unpack
the years of internalised homophobia,

or the irrational fear
i still seem to have of someone assuming
that i'm gay.

it doesn't feel good.
i still catch myself shrinking.

## 'i don't think i'm straight'

i paint my kitchen cabinets,
all by myself,
because i hear that lesbians
are supposed to be good at diy.

turns out i'm not.

they come out splotchy
and streaked
and i hate the colour i picked

and i'm worried
that i'm not the right sort of gay.

i'm worried that i'm too feminine
and then i'm worried that i'm too masculine
and then i'm worried that i'm not enough of either.

does feeling like an imposter ever go away?

*true*

i'm not sure what i expected,
but i think i thought that coming out
just meant coming out
once,

not every time
i meet someone new and
every time
i speak to old friends.

you never really stop
coming out.

it becomes part of the script,
something you just have to adjust to.

because it isn't just an instagram post
or sitting my parents down over dinner.

it is telling the world
again and
again and
again.

and praying for a good reaction,
again and
again and
again.

'i don't think i'm straight'

with fingertips clutching cotton,
i dream of it—
meeting her.
spine rubbed raw
from the tossing and the turning,

i plead for her,
in every sense.
toes and thighs alike,
clenched.
loose hair caught
between shoulder and bed.

night sweats and day sweats and afternoon showers.
the longing is always there.
the desire never goes away.

*true*

i came out and no pretty ladies
immediately declared their love for me.

*what the fuck?*

no mascs fell to their knees at my feet,
no fems with their soft skin and septum piercings
asked to hold my hand,
no cat rescuing,
stick-and-poke flavoured,
carabiner-wielding lesbian baristas
even attempted to u-haul with me?

*what. the actual. fuck?*

what was it all for,
if not the opportunity
to finally love in peace,
to finally hold the hand
of someone i *actually* love,
in public?

oh it's not that easy,
you say?

*why not?*

'i don't think i'm straight'

why must i struggle before coming out,
struggle to come out,
and then also struggle after coming out?

i know that women do not owe me anything,
believe me,
unlike my male counterparts,
my lust for women is not superseded
by my desire of ownership over them.

i am not disillusioned into thinking that
i am entitled to anything,
let alone a girlfriend.

but i'd like one,
now that i wouldn't have to hide her away.
i'd like to show her off.

*true*

and just when i had almost given up on love,

she
shows
up.

'i don't think i'm straight'

i ask her if she likes girls
and she doesn't look at me like i am crazy.

we share this yearning.
we are the same.
we are outcasts and lovers of women
and scared, but okay.

she understands me.
she makes me feel like i won't
ever have to be alone again.

she's quite pretty, isn't she?

*true*

i wish i had kissed her.
that night,
in her car.
i wish i'd had the courage i have now
and i wish i'd just
done
it.

she looked kissable,
she looked at me like i was kissable,
so why the fuck didn't i kiss her?
stupid, stupid me.
i hate how she makes me nervous.

## 'i don't think i'm straight'

she is unfortunate timing and soft skin and
dark hair
(because i won't admit it,
but i do have a type).

she is years of fictional love poems
unpublished and unread,
that i have written,
for no one in particular,
but somehow it was always her eye
i drew in the margins.

she is prayers,
mouthed silently into my pillowcase,
a lifetime of hope
bound in cotton bedsheets
and dreams.

she is who i used to see on every train,
at every street corner,
on buses and in airports
and my instagram's recommended accounts to follow.

she is funny and clever and a little bit wittier than me.
she makes me like myself
more than i ever thought i could

*true*

she was—is—
real,
both then and now,
and i have found her,
as alive
as i am.

cheeks pink
and mouth full of mine.

'i don't think i'm straight'

when it finally happens,
when the stars finally align,
it takes less than a second for her lips to find mine.

months of frustration
and tension
and hunger
has been poured into these mouths.
our hands find each other

and stay there.

*true*

you would love her,
you really would.

if you were still around to meet her,
you'd tell me to invite her round for a cuppa.
you'd bring out the best china,
the posh loose tea,
you'd make her feel so welcome,
you really would.

i wish you were still here to meet her.

'i don't think i'm straight'

she is easy to write lovely things for.
kissing me kindly,
she places her lips onto mine
and a thousand love poems
can be written.

she gives me enough inspiration to never need
skin again.
oh but i want it.
i would quite like it constantly.

*true*

tell me you feel this to.
oh
tell me.
press your heart against mine and let us forget where my
blood starts
and yours ends.

i beat for you
all mess and worry—
you have forged love
out of these wringing wrists
and fear is not something i am scared of anymore.

'i don't think i'm straight'

not the first.

not the first to make me squirm.
not the first to hold my hand and feel my heartbeat in my fingers.
not the first girl i have liked.

but the first who hasn't asked me to keep us a secret.
the first to be okay with how petrified i am,
with how anxious i am.
the first to touch me
and not make me feel bad about it after.

*true*

there is hatred living here among us.
it has crawled into our bed
and has tucked itself under
our chins.

sheets rucked, covered flesh, warmed, spoilt—
we are too much to each other.

and under the light from the next room over,
fingers wrap around skin
we would not touch
if it was our own.
we would not dare to be that brave.

i never thought i would fall in love with someone as
sick as myself,

but i am spoon-feeding you
and refusing the fork you place into my mouth.

sharpness exists here.
emptiness.
starvation.
cold bones and unwashed hair and brittle fingernails.
unkept, but still desired.

'i don't think i'm straight'

this thing—
this love—
this body as unwanted as my own,

it is making me hungry again.

i love you almost enough to save myself.
i love you almost enough to feed myself.
do you?

do
you?

*true*

i like me better in your dreams.
not by much,
but just enough to not hate myself.

## 'i don't think i'm straight'

when i walk past her in the mirror, when i see her and decide to, for the first time in a long while, actually look at her properly, i do not recognise her.

she is older, her hair is longer than i remember, her eyes more green. she looks happier, quieter. she is wearing rings and trousers that actually fit her waist. i think she has stopped squeezing herself into a size ten just because the number makes her feel something. i think she knows a number is just a number now. she has tattoos, fun hair, glasses. she is not wearing makeup,

and i wonder what changed, why now she seems so much more herself than she ever has. has she always had a smile that crooked? that real? she is human and beautiful and how the fuck have i never seen this before?

she does not recognise me, not at first, but she takes notice of me. she sees between my confusion and my trousers that fit and my red hair and the butterfly on my forearm and she holds out a hand to me, palm wide and fingers splayed. it is cold, flat, two dimensional. we touch but not really. we smile at each other but not really. i leave, look back and so does she. head tilted over my shoulder, body twisted, begging to live in this moment of self-love for just a little longer. i understand it better now.

i even look lovely as i walk away.

*true*

'i don't think i'm straight'

romantic love is nothing
if you do not also love yourself.

enough.
enough of the self-hatred.
you have grown past it.

it is time to start being kind to yourself.

*true*

she didn't cause this,
she wasn't one of the men who damaged me,
she is just a woman dealing with the consequences.

and i cannot stop apologising.
i am so sorry that
she has to be the one to deal with the repercussions,
to spoon-feed me enough love
to bring me back to health.

this wound in my heart
is going to be a part of me
for a very long time.

my poor younger self,
so confused,
so unhappy
and so unaccepted.

i would do anything to save her from the men that never held her best interests at heart.

'i don't think i'm straight'

love me with consideration.
i have been hurt far too many times to be held by
rough hands.
i am soft.
my heart is soft.
be kind to me.

*true*

i want you.
entirely and completely,
i want you.

on every good day
and every bad day
and every really, really shitty day,
i want you.

the days where we can't get out of bed together,
i want to lay next to you
and touch every inch of your skin with mine
and tell you
tomorrow is going to be better.

i want you to show me your favourite songs
and pretend that i like them,
or that i already know them,
and i want to show you mine
and have you do the same.

i want to kiss you in public,
in a library,
in the park,
in my favourite coffee shop,
like nobody else is sat there watching.

'i don't think i'm straight'

i want to cook pasta with you,
at three am in my kitchen,
while we dance,
badly.

i want to live with you
and i don't mean just live with you,
but experience life with you,
i want to live with you.
i want to do all of my living with you.

i want to clean my teeth with you,
wash my face with you,
brush my hair with you,
i want to shower with you.

i want you.

i don't even care if you want me back,
i just
want you.

*true*

tell me you'll never leave me.
promise me you want to stay.

here—
with our green bedsheets and cat-fur-covered comforters.

here—
with sleepily clasped hands and fingers so tangled,
we wake not recognising our own.

here—
with our open eyes
and open hearts
and bodies begging for safe love, for stability
not often granted
to twenty-somethings like us.

oh tell me this is a forever,
a scary, heavy enough to weigh us down
and drown us
forever.

a lovesick,
put me out of my misery,
i have never been so fulfilled

forever.

safe

'i don't think i'm straight'

i have a heart and i am not afraid to use it.

take that, homophobes.

*safe*

*i am queer.*
*i am queer.*
*i am queer.*

i will say it
because there was a time where i could not bring myself to.

i will say it
because there are still girls who do not know how to.

i will say it
because there were so many before me
who were not allowed to.

i will say it
because if i do not, who will say it for me?

i am queer and i am no longer ashamed.

'i don't think i'm straight'

time passes, attitudes change,
and break-ups that you never thought would happen,
happen.

and you keep moving.
and the world keeps spinning
and you feel more at home in your bones
than you ever thought you could.

you pick up new hobbies,
like adult dance classes
and you meet women who would literally
murder a man for you.

you meet new people—
some that you fall in love with,
some that make you wish you were dead again.
some that do both.

and you sort of enjoy it.
the journey,
the human-ness,
it makes you feel not alone,
which, really, is all you've ever wanted.

sure, you stay hoping,
keep an eye out for that magic we call love,
but you're whole already.

you like yourself. you really do.

*safe*

and although i have finally come to terms with my sexuality,
i cannot lie to you and say i welcomed it.

i had many pages filled with
angry scribbles
and teardrop stains that smudged my confessions.

i was honest,
but i was self-loathing.

then again,
i do not know
a single teenager who isn't.

'i don't think i'm straight'

some days,
i am still afraid.
i don't think that ever goes.

i still google whether a country is safe
to hold my girlfriend's hand in,
before i buy the plane tickets.

i still look around
and hesitate,
before i kiss her in public.

i still have to remind myself
that i am not dirty
or wrong
or a bad person.

i still forget to be proud
and unashamed
and to not hate the parts of me i cannot change.

i think about introducing her as a friend sometimes,
and not the love of my life,
if it means we won't have to spend the entire evening
explaining who the man is in the relationship.

i use the word partner,
not girlfriend,

*safe*

for protection.
because it is not technically a lie,
but it is not my truth.

i fantasise about how my life would be
if i could just push the gay in me
all the way down
and make a man happy,

but then i remember kissing that boy in year eight.

and i think about
how i had to wash my mouth out right after,
how i could feel his tongue
trickling down the back of my throat
for weeks after.

i remember brushing my teeth until i spat blood.

'i don't think i'm straight'

how sad it is
that something all about love
can create so much hate.

*safe*

sometimes i still hate this wretched skin
and this womanhood
and this love that i was forced to believe in
but no man has ever been able to provide for me.
i still hate this feminine hopefulness i have never been able
to burn out of me
and the kindness i taught myself
but will be expected to teach my son.

i still hate that when he predictably,
inevitably,
does not inherit the good feminist qualities i am burdened
with providing,
it will be my fault,

and my daughter,
who i will never have to sit down and ask not to rape her
future husband,
will practise empathy without prodding.
and i know she will only ever be subject to the same fate as
myself.

i still hate this horrid,
unstoppable cycle of life and death
and forgiveness
that is embedded into my body.

## 'i don't think i'm straight'

and sometimes i still want to,
gently,
gouge out my organs in a ladylike manner
and replace them with dirt and flowers and everything alive
so that i may feel like less of a carcass.

just give me an hour of peace from this hatred taught to me,
i beg,
an hour.

an hour of not being a woman,
surrounded by men.

oh lord, please believe me,
i do not want to hate men,

but surely there would be more peace for us
if they did not exist?
if they were not angrily slamming down toasters
and picking open bathroom locks?

i do not want to be a bad feminist.
i do not want to be the butt of every man's joke.
i do not want to be just another crazy female who's a bit too high-strung.
i do not want to be another statistic,
another reason for men to hate women,
another 'too loud', 'too intense', 'too difficult'
to deal with.

*safe*

i want to wear a floor-length dress
and i want to be angry
and i want to scream
and i want to laugh so hard, i sob
and i do not want a single person to touch or pity me
ever again.

i want to eat blueberries
until my fingertips are stained purple
and i want to care so little that later,
when i find my prints on my dress,
i add more out of sheer defiance.

i want warmth in my heart and
softness under my bare feet
and i want only women to love me.

i want every man's eyes to miss me when i walk past.
i want to be invisible to them,
a ghost in my femininity.

i want to,
purposefully,
drive until i am lost,
without a man in my passenger seat, problem-solving my
non-problem.

'i don't think i'm straight'

i want to be listened to
and understood
and heard.
and i want other women to wake up
and put on their floor-length dress
and eat their fruit
and drive their cars
and i want us to laugh together.

i want us to laugh together
so hard,
that we sob together, too.

*safe*

safety comes in numbers.
remember that,
the next time you think being alone
might be easier.

it's not.

you have sisters you have never even met,
siblings waiting for you to wake up
and join them,
to find your community
and figure out what home is.

you're safe with them. they'll look after you.

they'll teach you how to put on eyeliner,
how to tell a man to fuck off
and not feel guilty about it.

they'll be beautiful
and scary
and wholly themselves.

and they won't apologise for it.
they aren't ashamed.

you can be like them, if you let yourself.
if you give into the desire, and the fear.

you can be everything you've always wanted to be.

'i don't think i'm straight'

they either learnt to accept me,
or they didn't.

either way,
i ended up surrounded by only the loveliest of people.

*safe*

she was not the first girl i fell in love with.
it was not all new and exciting and clumsy teenage emotion.

it was real
and adult
and safe.

i was not afraid to be seen holding her hand in town.
we kissed waiting for the bus.
she put her hand on my thigh over dinner.

people stared.
i felt sorry for them.
they must not understand love.

'i don't think i'm straight'

how could something

this sweet

deserve to be

frowned upon?

*safe*

when we hold hands,
our palms pressed tightly in prayer,
i believe in a god again.
i believe in butterflies and bile and dandelions
and i make wish after wish
until i taste sour in my mouth.

i have never understood
how a person could be sick with love.
how could something so good for me
possibly make me even a little bit unwell?

i look at her and i want to vomit.

i'm serious, i do.
full chest and empty stomach,
i look at her
and it is enough to make me empty my guts
and open my heart.

i want to clean between my bones for her,
rip skin from the inside of my throat,
i vow to purge the everyone except her
out of my body.

without gentleness,
rough and angry and begging for forgiveness,
i hate myself for ever not loving her.

'i don't think i'm straight'

i want to rid myself of any flesh
any person but her
has ever known.

she has never asked for it,
she is too good for that,
but how can i look at her
and want to give her anything other than
pleasure?

she touches me and
how dare i have ever let anyone else
before her.

she kisses me and
how could i have ever used this mouth
for anything else.

*safe*

every past version of me knows you.

i swear,
i went back
and whispered your name
into their ears.

## 'i don't think i'm straight'

she sees how i flinch when i am not freshly showered,
she wonders why i go on and on about being unclean,
and she asks me to tell her why,
to tell her about my past.

she holds me in the crooks of her arms while i sob,
repeats many times how it is okay
that there were others before her,
that i am worth more
than what they told me i was.

she makes me a rooibos tea,
i hope i can love myself more tomorrow.

she braids my hair,
it lays flat out of my face,
she tells me i am gorgeous.

never have i been so safe.
never have i felt so accepted.
this is good,
this is nice.
this is healthy.

*safe*

i love her.
sickeningly.
she gives me tooth rot.

'i don't think i'm straight'

she has cleaned me,
softened my stray hairs
and made me more presentable.

she knows when to touch my lower back
and when to kiss my sorry lips.

i cry and she cries too.
tears filled with love
remind us of how sweet each other's taste.

but oh how i am thankful to wipe hers away.

*safe*

galaxies,
i swear,
there are galaxies in the bedsheets among us.
bold and quiet, calm and beautiful,
the way she kisses my shoulders
makes me think of heaven.

soft body, softer heart,
she could pierce me
if she tried hard enough,

my skin would fold itself
neatly in front of her if
she asked it to.
she would not even have to say
please.

oh but she would,
wouldn't she?
and she would say thank you, too.

'i don't think i'm straight'

long deserving of a sweetness like this,
nothing compares to the love of a woman.

she has cradled my inner child, comforted
and warmed.

the validation is easy,
and i think overdue.

there are no whispers of power imbalances,
no need to mention manipulation,
or raise our voices.

the healing i have found
in loving this woman
is unmatched.

years of torment
and unhappiness
has led to this,
to her.

it was all worth it,
every damn second of it.

she is most definitely worth it.

*safe*

oh how good it feels

to not be

ashamed.

'i don't think i'm straight'

i hear her speak
and i forget how heavy my tongue is
in my mouth.

weightless.

and nothing else matters
and everyone else melts away
and it is just us,
sat across from each other,
speaking words
we have always been too scared to say.
this is power.

i don't feel the tears on my cheeks
until i taste them.
oh look at how much you have made me
feel.

*safe*

my rug sits pretty
on my stone floor
and i kiss her
laying on it.

it is second hand,
worn thin
and well loved—

nothing cushions our bodies
except love.
i would not have it
any other way.

'i don't think i'm straight'

kiss me,
you pretty thing, you—

petal skin
warmed heart
lovely mouthed
thing, you—

brown lashed
kindly handed
favourite jumper thing, you—

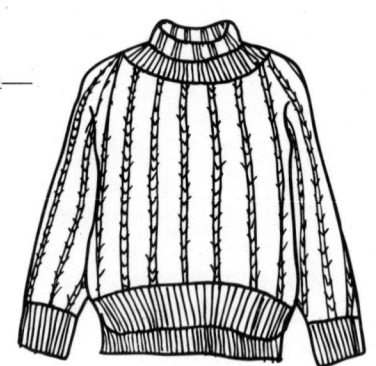

little lover
light sleeper
purse holder
thing, you—

are all
i have ever
wanted.

you pretty thing, you.

the funny thing about sleeping in bed with someone
you love,
is that while the night-times contain sex
and
passion

*safe*

and
open-mouthed kissing,

it's the mornings that are by far

the most intimate.

waking up and holding them,
touching every inch of their skin
with yours,

trying not to spill the coffee they made you
on your freshly washed bedding.

'i don't think i'm straight'

and i swear on everything,
i've found god there.

hipbone-dented cheeks
and sore mouths
and cracked backs—

in between the sex and the kissing and the laying,
god is there.

something exists and it is good.
it has made me thankful for this woman,
for the burden i was given of loving my own gender.

god is real and i believe this now and i kiss her again.

*safe*

never has a man made me
this happy.

never.

'i don't think i'm straight'

her hair falls on my shoulders
and i like how our rings sound
when we touch
each other.

scary, isn't it?

to be everything
you spent years hiding from.
to fill the shoes the mean girls at school
noticed you wearing
before you did.

i didn't even know what a dyke was
until they called me one.

and comp-het is a funny thing,
isn't it?
to learn my attraction is not my own
like i thought it was,
to learn it was never mine
to begin with.

i suppose it's all just disney's fault anyway,
a teacher's fault letting boys
chase me around the playground,
my mum's for asking me

*safe*

when i was finally going to bring a boy home.

she smells like pistachios, you know?
nutty and sweet and
like a baked good,
before it's been baked.

i don't know how they knew,
those girls,
the mean ones,
but they did.
they knew about us all,

because it's funny how the
'*not-quite-out-yets*'
all tend to group together over lunch,

how every month
since leaving school,
someone else seems to come out.

facebook posts,
hard launches of their girlfriends,
'*my first day on hormones*' videos on my feed.

you lose touch,
you don't eat your sandwiches
in the art room
together anymore,

## 'i don't think i'm straight'

but you don't lose the feeling of
community.

because we were there,
before anyone else was,
we were safe and scared,
but hidden.

we were secrets
and whispers of

     *'is this normal?'*
and

     *'i don't think i'm straight'*
and

     *'do you like it when i touch you here?'*

i think she's fallen asleep on me.
her chest rises and my feet are numb
and our hands
do not let go.

sunlight hits our disco ball,
which hits our houseplants
and tapestries
and cats

*safe*

(because we are gay women,
of course we have cats).

it is sweet,
being sapphic,
being everything
i was supposed to be,
i am not ashamed.
i am not a secret.

i am out and i am not dead and i am in love.

with
a
woman.

# acknowledgements

my reading goal for 2025 is to read over 100 books. as of writing this, i am most definitely behind schedule.

my favourite part of any book is the acknowledgements. it feels like a proper fourth-wall break, a moment for the author to look directly into the camera and write as themselves for once. i love it. and that's why writing them is also my least favourite thing to do.

there's an immense amount of pressure to 'get it right', to never forget anyone, to spell everyone's surnames correctly and, most importantly, to submit it in time for print (which, i have just about done).

i'm never sure what tone to take, if i should be earnest, funny, kind, or to the point. i've debated foregoing them altogether out of decision paralysis, but it doesn't make sense to love something so much that you just refuse to do it. and every book needs acknowledgements, it is an unavoidable fact of life (and of publishing). so, here we go.

thank you to every queer activist, and every LGBTQIA+ icon, who paved the way for people like me to write books

# acknowledgements

like this. thank you for how you fought for us, and i hate that you ever had to.

thank you to the entire team at ebury that i've had the pleasure of working with, i really do have the best publishers. a special thank you to sam crisp, my editor, who listened to all the silly ideas i had about this book, and turned them into something magic.

thank you to the poets i have been lucky enough to bring along on my live poetry tours, bradley taylor, m. l. walsh, becca lloyd, jack lawrence, emily weaver, pril wood, áine ní néil, liam campbell, lauren gillespie, moon churchill anna doran, alys lloyd, carol forrester and aisha akram, plus many, many more who have shared the stage during our open mics. i really should name you all but i think we'd run out of ink.

thank you to my family and my friends, for listening to my late-night rambles and for always being my guinea pigs when it comes to making decisions about books covers. thank you for loving me and accepting me and helping me learn who i am. especially you mum, you're my favourite cheerleader.

thank you to every reader whose favourite part of any book is also the acknowledgements. i like you. a lot. everyone else doesn't know what they're missing.

and a finally, big old thank you to my followers on social media. i'm only here writing this because of you. i am so unbelievably grateful for this job and the life you have given me. i can't imagine ever doing anything else.

until the next acknowledgements, i'll see you then. x

## about the author

isabella dorta is a poet and author living in somerset, england, with her three cats and her many, many houseplants. isabella published her first collection, *how sunflowers bloom under moonlight* on valentines day 2022, after a very silly man broke her very heavy heart. known for reading her poetry aloud on social media, she posted her first poem online in may 2021 and has carefully built a loving community of followers. she has since gone on to publish five more poetry collections, as well as hosted three sold-out poetry tours, which, in her words, goes to show 'that really, all the best things come out of spite.'

@isabelladortapoetry444
on tiktok and instagram